At the Edge
of the
Cities Burning

At the Edge of the Cities Burning

Mattie McClane

Myrtle Hedge Press

Copyright © 2023
Myrtle Hedge Press, Kure Beach, North Carolina

ISBN 978-1-7329970-3-5
Library of Congress Control Number 2022951427

Design by Val Sherer, Personalized Publishing Services
Photo 13788239 © Zatletic | Dreamstime.com

To my husband, John Kaiser

Preface

I am writing this preface near the third Sunday of Advent, which comes December 11 in 2022. Advent is a time of anticipation, a time when Catholic Church liturgy focuses on a second coming of Jesus Christ. I have become a woman who waits for the new kingdom. I can think of nothing more important to do than to hope for peace and a coming together of adversaries.

The Russian-Ukrainian War, the reality of climate change, both prompt uncertain times and cast shadows on daily life. In this small book, I explore the darker side of the early 21st Century's current events, as well as the glory of the Triune God, a God that was revealed to me when I audited the fall class, "The Mystery of the Trinity," at Boston College's School of Theology and Ministry.

Rafael Luciani, the brilliant Venezuelan theologian taught the online class, and his reflections were so deep that the only way I could find a sufficient response to them was through poetry. With verse, I became articulate.

Yet, let me be clear. *At the Edge of the Cities Burning* are my thoughts, with the concerns I have touched on throughout my writing career. It might shock some readers, even Christians to mention hell. Still, I am convinced that there are inherent sorry effects when we deny God's essence or ethics and do not promote the well-being of humanity and creation; people's souls are accountable. The world yearns for a humankind that knows there are consequences for actions.

Finally, readers might wonder if *At the Edge of the Cities Burning* is political or religious. It depends upon the lens in which the poem is read; the politico will see politics, while disciples will grasp its religious scope. The poem has been called both, "depressing" and "beautiful." Its effects are in the "eye of the beholder," which is why I consider it an important work for the era.

–Mattie McClane
Wilmington, NC

At the Edge
of the
Cities Burning

I.

"The Spirit of the Lord is upon me.
because he has anointed me
to bring glad tidings to the poor.
He has sent me to proclaim liberty
to the captives, and recovery of sight
to the blind and let the oppressed
go free and to proclaim a year
acceptable to the Lord."

Rolling up the scroll, he handed it back
to the attendant and sat down. All in the
synagogue had their eyes fixed on him.

– Luke 4:18-20

I looked into
the eyes
of a working poet

and found
a peaceful soul
the calm
from saying
from witnessing
the world
as it is,
hard
but truthful
facts.
Later, an old lady
told me she
was taken
by the Holy Spirit
one day
while ironing. She
did not tell me
if it was a skirt

or blouse
that she straightened
only that her mind
and body
were filled
with joy. This,
while the world
was burning.
the orange fire of missiles
crowding
the tube's screen
this desert storm,
where men
would die.
Of course,
there were commercials
interruptions
from the faraway

unfelt pain. So
why is
the poet
calm and why
does
the elderly
woman tell me
of her bliss?

Tell me what
is to be done
when people
only love
slightly,
narrowly
their own? Humanity
might take
action, protest

the waste
the desolation
of souls. I am
a poet who
has loved much
and looked
on hell
felt the distress
the extreme discomfort
and prayed
to that chain-cutter
the God of wisdom
and freedom.

I am restless
with an ardent desire
of radiant light
seeing

its shadows
my fingers
type, and I know
that the forces
of good and harm
are palpable
It's no Sunday
preacher's dream
no dishonest
ploy for loose change
or greenbacks
to obtain power
each with followers
who both cry
for the word justice.

I recognize my privilege
my situation

my elite station,
and I wonder
if I can tell
this story.
I have watched
the hellish clock
the *same* time
that is *kept*
in nursing *homes*
and prisons.
The hands
change
slowly,
and one waits
throughout
seeming eternity
for one visitor
who looks sane

or who might
not yell
out at night
about thieves
and intruders
or who can
carry on
a friendly conversation.

For 25 years
I zeroed in on
the public realm
to see
if I could find
and tell
what
is hidden.
You'll have

to surmise
to guess
at the real motive
the true
beneficiaries
for most
official actions.
Here comes
the saying
that advises
one to ignore
offered plans
in favor
of what
people do.
Watch,
realizing folks
are incapable

of saving
themselves
in present time.
They wait
for history
the narration
the compass
that is too late
they are repentant
sorry for crimes
the tipping
point
of environmental
calamity
reported
by yesterday's
scientists
prophets

who are cold,
preserved
in their graves.

The prophets
are mediators
revealing
the divine
presence
of the unbegotten
who hears
the cries
of the poor
many stories
within the great one.
You will know
the vocation
when books

are banned. When
the gatekeepers
edit and erase
treatises
taking words out
of context
or simply
confiscating texts
on the way
to archives.
She/he/they
will be the target
of ridicule
of harassment
given the option
of obscurity
or death
while at

the edge of
the cities' burning.

II.

The people in the synagogue were
furious when they heard this. They got
up, drove him out of town, and took him
to the edge of the hill on which their city
was built, in order to throw him off the cliff.
But he walked right through the crowd and
went on his way.

– Luke 4:28-30

The old woman
cleaned
the oak pews
after services
at a little
church known
as a wedding
venue in Iowa.

She told me
that she waited
for Jesus.
to come back
for a second time.
I was a young 30
dismissing
the statement
as a common
elderly wish.
After all, what
was she to look
forward to
at her age?
When she died,
they found
news clips in her Bible.

the fossil fuels
are burning
the forests
are burning
the vineyards
are burning
the oceans
are burning
the coral reefs
are burning
the mountains
are burning
the houses
are burning
the businesses
are burning
the corporations
are burning

the cities
are burning.

The aggressor says
America set
the precedent
for nuclear war
with Hiroshima
and Nagasaki.
When is military might
called just?
The powerful
make soldiers
of fathers
and sons
mothers
and daughters:
for what gain?

The borders
are expanded
as is the survivors'
hatred. The
political realm
is the search
the constant aim
for advantage
the upper hand
for how many members
are in legislatures
the consuming
high lifestyles
of wealthy white men.

I looked into the eyes
of a great
theologian

and found
a humble spirit.
He says God
wants people
to live in relationship
in community.
How radical
is the call
for the humanization
of people
who would be
not perfect
but more perfect
because of Christ.
The essence
of the Triune God
is wholeness
and unity,

the three are one.
God is the God
of time
before time.
God is the God
of history
before history
God is the God
of creation
before creation.
God is the God
of the poor
before the poor
God is the God of
language
before language.

God is the God of love
no beginning
and no end.

You'll not listen
to wise people
who seem
to know
how the world
should be.
The Spirit
put tongues
of flame above
the heads
of holy disciples
and in everyday
language
all language

followers spread
the lessons
of the poor
from the transcendent
the begotten
Word, the hope
for the reign
of the new kingdom.
The old order
will pass away.
Let it pass away.

III.

The apartment
building's units
are left
without walls
like doll houses
in the nursery
the view
of homes
abandoned
torn, fluttering
insulation
broken drywall
once thoughtful decor
domestic
spaces open
to the wind.
Below,

the dogs circle
the warzone
they amble
through
the soot-layered grass
smoky skies
blue mornings
in search
of masters
missing
who have fled
with families
grandmothers
unsuspecting
children
with backpacks
carrying toys
all in a hurry

to escape
the missiles
the sirens
the explosions
with the instinct to live.

the coal
is burning.
the oil
is burning.
the Artic
is burning.
North
America
is burning.
Europe
is burning.
Africa

is burning.
Asia
is burning.
South
America
is burning.
Australia
is burning.
Antarctica
is burning.
continents
are burning.

I looked into
the eyes
of a public servant
and saw
a heart

and mind
recognizing
the potential
to connect
humankind.
Ballots
are testimonies,
the many voices
brought
to the table.
With popular
rule, there
are options
choices
for practical action
for compassion,
a tender
nurturing

feeling

for the planet

using

experiences

of place

of time

of history

to include

others

into a larger story.

Walt Whitman

thought

democracy

promotes

brotherhood.

Many folks

share a bond

through a
benevolent
government
system, where
each person
counts
and is afforded
God-given dignity.

Jane Addams
a social reformer,
wanted
democracy
to be more
than a vote
but a way
of living,
complete

social ethics
an appreciation
of knowledge
of diverse stories.

The essence
of the Triune God
is equality,
the three
are equal.
God is the God
of fairness
no beginning
and no end.
God is the God
of inclusion
no beginning
and no end

God is the God
of truth
no beginning
and no end.
God is the God
of justice
no beginning
and no end.
God is the God
of mercy
no beginning
and no end.
God is the God
of peace
no beginning
and no end
God is the God
of freedom

no beginning
and no end.

People begin
to journey
to walk
to escape war's
destruction,
uninhabitable
land. They
congregate
in border
towns
at outdoor
kitchens
with soup kettles
the luxury
of hot food

of charity.
They gather
near water
to wash dirty
clothes
the smell
of sweat
is everywhere
at only the start
of the world's
movement.

High temperatures
extreme
weather
kill the crops,
the rice
is burning

the wheat
is burning.
the corn
is burning.
the flax
is burning
the barley
is burning
the oats
are burning
the soybeans
are burning.
the vegetables
are burning.
the grasslands
are burning.

You'll not listen
to teachers
to farmers
to pastors
to thinkers
to scientists
who seem
to know how
the world
should be. You
will want
to deny
or adapt
to crisis.
Folks cannot
save themselves
in present time.
Families will

migrate
when fields
are dry
and crack
looking like puzzle
pieces.

I looked into
the eyes
of an ordinary
woman
and saw
every woman,
her second-rate status
her concerns
about oppression
and violence
at home

in the workplace
She is not free
or equal
in her own
relationships
and communities.

The aggressor's army
is pushed back
losing
territory.
Officials
discuss
using nuclear
weapons.
Will they sooner
or later?
With winter

coming,
they strike infrastructure
power sources.
The people prepare
to suffer
in the cold
and dark.
The cities
are burning.
The world
might become
a battlefield.

Tokyo
is burning.
Delhi
is burning.
Shanghai

is burning
Sao Paulo
is burning
Mexico City
is burning
Beijing
is burning.
Osaka
is burning.
New York
is burning.

IV.

"I, John saw another angel come up from the East, holding the seal of the living God. He cried out in a loud voice to the four angels who were given power to damage the land and the sea. 'Do not damage the land, the sea or the trees until we put the seal on the heads of the servants of our God...' After this I had a vision of a great multitude which no one could count, from every nation, race, people, and tongue. They stood before the throne and the lamb... They cried out in a loud voice,
'Salvation comes from our God, who is seated on the throne and from the Lamb'"

– Rev. 7:2-4

I looked into the spirit
of a living God
and found
a companion
and a liberator
who frees humankind
from mistakes
who restores
shattered places
making new
a broken world.

About the Author

Mattie McClane is an American novelist, poet, and journalist. She is the second and youngest daughter born to James L. and Shirlie I. Myers in Moline, Illinois. Her father was a commercial artist and her mother worked as a secretary.

McClane's earliest education was in the Catholic schools. Her experience with their teachings deeply affected her. At a young age, she became aware of gender inequality. She credits her early religious instruction for making her think about "all kinds of truths and ethical matters."

McClane's parents divorced when she was eight years old. Her mother remarried attorney John G. Ames and the new couple moved to a house beside the Rock River. The river centrally figures in McClane's creative imagination. She describes her childhood as being "extraordinarily free and close to nature."

McClane moved to Colorado and married John Kaiser in 1979 in Aurora, just East of Denver.

They then moved to Bettendorf, Iowa, where they had three children. John worked as a chemist. Mattie became interested in politics, joining the local League of Women Voters. According to McClane, she spent her 20s "caring for young children and working for good government."

She graduated from Augustana College with a B.A. degree in the Humanities. She began writing a political column for Quad-Cities Online and Small Newspaper Group, based in Illinois.

Her family moved to Louisville, Kentucky where she continued with her journalism and then earned an M.A. in English from the University of Louisville. Critically acclaimed author Sena Jeter Naslund directed her first creative thesis, "Unbuttoning Light and Other Stories," which was later published in a collection.

She was accepted to the University of North Carolina at Wilmington's M.F.A. in Creative Writing Program, where she wrote the short novel *Night Ship*, working under the tutelage of Pulitzer Prize winning author Alison Lurie. McClane studied with Dennis Sampson in poetry also. She graduated in 1999.

She would write a column for the *High Point Enterprise* in North Carolina. She would later write for the *News and Observer.* McClane has regularly published commentary for over 25 years.

Mattie McClane is the author of *Night Ship: A Voyage of Discovery* (2003, 2017), *River Hymn: Essays Evangelical and Political* (2004), *Wen Wilson* (2009, 2022), *Unbuttoning Light: The Collected Short Stories of Mattie McClane* (2012), *Now Time* (2013), *Stations of the Cross* (2016), *The Mother Word, An Exploration of the Visual* (2017), *Simeon's Canticle* (2018), *The Song of the Grackle* (2019), *The Magnificent Light of Morning* (2021), *To Free the Sisters of Mary* (2022), *At the Edge of the Cities' Burning* (2023).

She lives in North Carolina.